The Put the YOU in IoT Handbook

Everyone's Guide to the Internet of Things

Jerrold Clifford

&

Steven Clifford

© copyright 2020 Jerrold Clifford

All rights reserved

ISBN: 9781700350206

First Printing: 2020 Printed in the United States of America

The Put the YOU in IoT Handbook is available for bulk orders, special orders and premiums. For details email: TheIoTHandbook@gmail.com

About the Authors

Jerrold Clifford is the author of 6 books and numerous articles. After graduating from New York's famed Bronx High School of Science he earned his BS degree from the Polytechnic Institute of Brooklyn and his Masters degree in mathematics from SUNY at Stony Brook. He has certifications in IT audit and project management and is a past President of the NJ chapter of the Information Security Audit and Control Association (ISACA). He is the recipient of an award from the President of the United States.

Jerrold combined this with an extensive computer technology, IT background and business experience and became known as *The Project Manager Screwdriver* because he takes projects which are screwed up and "unscrews" them. He applies this unique background to solving IoT project challenges.

Steven Clifford can be described as a product claims verifier – he specializes in taking manufacturer's claims about their products and verifying their accuracy. He built on his educational background in marketing working with product demonstrators to show individual consumers the benefits of particular products. Recognizing that manufacturers also need product credibility, he performs product testing in his "home laboratory". Both corporate and individual consumers seek his recommendations for IoT product implementation strategies and coordinating mixed IoT platform product usage.

The authors may be contacted at author@theiothandbook.com

Introduction

The internet, unheard of by most people just a few years ago, is actually over 40 years old and is now utilized by those individuals, businesses, even governments countless times each day. It refers to a global computer arrangement which enables people to communicate with each other and consists of interconnected networks incorporating standardized communication protocols. The idea arose that if people could communicate with each other, why couldn't the concept be extended to communication with, and between, devices.

- **Thus, was born the concept of** the "INTERNET OF THINGS (IoT)."

IoT devices are now being used both in the home and commercial places.
Some examples of devices that utilize this concept include:
- Home lighting that can be operated via a smart phone, home heating, and air conditioning controls and devices, illumination controls and lights, appliances, entertainment systems, security approaches, and irrigation methods.
- Home devices including temperature, lighting, and security devices, pet and commercial livestock devices (such as collars for monitoring animals).
- Commercially, power distribution, agriculture, municipal operations, transportation, hospitality and financial services exemplify just a few of the sectors where **IoT** is interrupting and transforming how business is accomplished.
- The **IoT** concept has opened to the development of marketable items that until recently were not even imagined as practical.
- Some of these items include health and sports-related clothes, such as shirts, watches, and armbands that provide biometric information.
- Transportation industry controls for monitoring planes, trains, cars, and passenger movement, city-supplied service management controls, and health care support.

Previously it would have taken the mystical crystal ball to predict the future. However now a quick visit to the internet shows new items with **IoT properties** being offered every day. How we perform tasks in the present is being disrupted to be replaced by **IoT**–centric processes and equipment. It doesn't take magic to determine that a few of the new areas where IoT will be expanded include clothing where wearable sports and exercise monitoring is already being built in, unmanned vehicles (driverless cars are currently being tested and **IoT** devices are finding their way onto planes, trains and boats), medicine where **IoT** technology is being incorporated into surgical robots and *environment surveillance* (illegal logging and animal poaching detection). Medically, devices ae being developed to monitor patients and even perform surgery remotely.

While the exact number can't be established It has been projected that there will be in the neighborhood of 22.5 billion **IoT** devices in 2021 and almost $5 trillion will be invested in **IoT** by companies between 2016 and 2021. The number of smart home products and services on the market steadily and rapidly and continuous large growth in recent years. In households with broadband, 26% of consumers own at least one smart home device. But, however rapidly the **IoT** landscape is changing there are still challenges that must be addressed. Some manufacturers use their own proprietary technology in designing their products; others use an "open" technology. Even where *open technology* is utilized, differences in standardization can make it difficult to communicate between products thereby requiring that a compatibility analysis be performed when constructing systems of linked products. The steps in determining compatibility requires deciding areas where interoperability conflicts might occur and how to resolve these issues can be confusing, costly, time consuming, and result in a need to compromise some desired functionality. Common standards which could aid this process have not been determined and product certifiability requirements need to be developed.

This book is designed to provide a basis for understanding **IoT**, serve as a reference for designing residential and commercial **IoT** systems and determining required information and vital factors for the selection and installation of **IoT** devices.

ACKNOWLEDGEMENTS

The authors would like to thank the experts and manufacturers who provided valuable information and material in making this book possible. Special thanks to:

Frank Kovacs for his unwavering guidance and support

Adelaida A. Rodriguez for her unsurpassed editing and encouragement

Pretam Sinur for consummate technical review and advice

Giannna Milia for her artistic talent

Caroline Shelby for her photography skills

and to

Carl E. Reid for his long time belief, inspiration and truly helping to make this book a reality.

This Book Is Dedicated To:

Rosa Veronika

and

Angela Samantha

The Deep Dive - What's Inside

Chapter 1

What better place to start than with the **basics**. The Internet of Things (IoT) is defined, how it works, **examples** and the **terminology** used to describe **IoT devices** and **environments** are provided. Since the **government** has an important role in assuring the success of IoT, governmental actions are included. **Blockchain** increasingly is being incorporated into the IoT space; what it is and how it is being utilized and its effect on IoT are explained. **Sensors** are critical in IoT devices; what they are, the different sensor categories and how they are utilized can be found here. Many companies have **legacy systems** and considerations for their conversion to IoT are discussed here.

Chapter 2

This chapter starts with **technology** basics and moves on to advanced topics. Factors which detailed include **communication**, **backbone**, **hardware**, **protocols**, **software**, **cloud platforms** and **machine learning**. IoT advantages and disadvantages including **security** and **social concerns** are addressed. Determining needs and requirements and both **machine learning** and **Obsolescence considerations** are detailed. **Commercial and individual environments**.

Chapter 3

Security and **privacy** are major IoT concerns. Capabilities of different communications **generations** are included. Exposures, design considerations, interfaces and backward compatibility issues are addressed. **Privacy concerns, vulnerabilities** both within new and legacy systems are addressed.

Chapter 4

Technical lifestyle and **help desk support concerns** for both manufacturers and customers are detailed. **Standards** needs, **modularity** in construction are discussed. **Smart cities** are described and **smart and smarter devices** are presented. **Energy optimization** and **geofencing** are included as are **self-diagnosing products** and **retail store** considerations.

Chapter 5

This chapter includes some **principle advances** being developed – the future. **Challenges facing companies** are addressed including **data mining**, **VR** considerations and implications, **medical advances, telecommunications, fabrics and wearables, jobs** and the **work environment** and **what's next**.

Appendix 1

This section deals with **the "how tos"** for both individuals and companies. Includes how to **assess needs**, how to **obtain IoT devices**, how **determine security**, how **to get devices to work together**, how to **deploy a successful IoT projects**.

Appendix 2

Devices which are available and device requirements.

Key IoT Terms

Terms that assist in understanding IoT concepts, development, installation and usage.

Table of Contents

The Deep Dive - What's Inside vi

Chapter 1 – Basics 1

What is the Internet of Things (IoT)? 1

    IoT Examples 3

    How IoT works 3

    IoT Technology 4

    Government Initiatives 5

    Blockchain 6

    How Blockchain Works 7

        The Effect of Blockchain on IoT 8

    Sensors 8

        Multiple purpose sensors and devices 9

    Categories of Sensors 9

    Legacy Concerns 10

Chapter 2 – Considerations when updating 13

    Technology Basics 13

    Radio Frequency Identification 14

    NFC 14

    Bluetooth 14

    Wi-Fi 14

    Backbone 16

Hardware 16

Protocols 16

Software 17

Cloud 17

Determining Needs and Requirements 21

Commercial 21

Company direction, objectives and goals 21

Plan for IoT Product Development 22

Usage in a Commercial Environment 23

Individual Considerations 24

Obsolescence considerations 25

Obsolescence Planning 26

Machine Learning 26

CHAPTER 3 – Security and Privacy 29

Communication between devices technology 29

Backward Compatibility 31

Design Considerations 32

Installation and Design considerations 33

Security 33

IoT Privacy Issues 33

Security Issues 36

Chapter 4 – Technical Lifestyle 39

Help Desk Support 39

Smart Cities 40

Security 40

Public vs. Private Networks 40

Smarter Devices 41

Optimization and Saving Energy 42

Self-Diagnosing Products 43

Retail Store Support 43

Chapter 5 – The Future 45

Transportation 45

Challenges facing companies 46

Support 46

Data Mining 46

VR considerations and future implications 47

Medical advances 48

Telecommunications 48

Fabrics and Wearables 48

Jobs and the Work Environment 49

What's next? 50

Appendix 1– The How To's 53

How To Obtain IoT Devices 53

Determining your objective 53

Establishing a budget 53

Determining wanted and needed devices 53

Obtaining the devices and getting them to work together 54

How to address IoT security 54

Corporate Environments 54

Individual Environments 55

How to Deploy a Successful IoT Project 56

Tips on How to Synchronize Whole Home Audio 57

Appendix 2 – Devices and IoT requirements 59
   Smart Bicycles and accessories 59
   Home Devices 60
   Heating & Cooling 61
      IOT Thermostats 61
   Lighting 63
   Security 64
Key IoT Terms 85

The Put the YOU in IoT Handbook

Chapter 1 – Basics

What is the Internet of Things (IoT)?

The term **internet** refers to a global computer arrangement of physical objects which enables people to communicate with each other. This arrangement consists of interconnected networks incorporating standardized communication protocols. Analogous to a land-based post office mail system which requires recipients and senders to have a unique mailing address for proper mail delivery, devices to have connection to the internet must have a unique address for communication to work properly. This is called an **Internet Protocol (IP) address**. **Internet of Things (IoT)** refers to networks of physical objects with an IP address coupled with the communication that occurs between them and other Internet-enabled devices and systems and utilizes interconnected networks incorporating standardized communication protocols.

Consumers and businesses are constantly updating their homes and buildings, work spaces or offices and even vehicles and surroundings with new gadgets and updated replacement items. Traditionally, manufacturers have focused on producing items as stand-alone objects. For example, light bulbs were designed with wattage, voltage, and color as design criteria. The requirement that they turn on to a voice command would only be a design requirement under special circumstances. Being able to operate in conjunction with another device wasn't even considered; to do so required physical connections such as wires and the ability to do this was constrained by factors such as distance, voltage, and current capacity and appearance.

Cooperation and coordination between manufacturers of different devices was required. This, in turn, meant the need to agree on interface design criteria.

The foundation for voice-activated devices was begun in the early 1980's with work on commercial deployment of cellular networks (*see chapter 3*). Work on voice-activated devices was performed early in the 21st century with some success but also with language-related issues. Ensuring that devices properly understood commands and did not inadvertently interpret ordinary words as executable commands were some of the difficulties. Developing the system that would eventually be called Amazon Echo began in 2011.

Cloud computing (also called **cloud services** or **remote computing services**) is a general term for the delivery of hosted services over the Internet. Knowing the workings of cloud technology is not a requirement but understanding some of the features of cloud computing is necessary to appreciate **IoT** capabilities.

There are multiple **IoT** cloud platforms. These include:
- Amazon Web Services
- Microsoft Azure
- Google cloud
- Heroku
- OpenStack

The cloud computing platform provided by Amazon.com is called **Amazon Web Services** (AWS). Web services were available in 2006.
- *Microsoft Azure* was released in 2010.
- *Google cloud storage* was introduced in 2010.
- *Heroku* supports several programming languages and was acquired by Salesforce.com in 2010.
- *OpenStack,* initially released in 2010 is free and provides an open-source software platform for cloud computing.

IoT Examples

Devices and applications that are included in the **IoT** category are varied and increasing in numbers daily. Examples include obvious items as well as things which affect our daily lives but may not be so apparent.

- Visual examples include connected security systems, driverless cars, heating and cooling system thermostats, electronic appliances, household and commercial lights, and entertainment speaker systems, vending machines and more.
- Behind the scenes items and systems include transportation tracking (passengers and equipment), city management (sanitation, water supply, and vehicle movement), health systems (organ monitoring, robotics).
- Data analytics is a process of examining, presenting and modeling data with the goal of determining information assisting in decision making.
- A combination of cloud, data management and **IoT** is being used to further data analytics capabilities enhancing company analysis of factors and components affecting production of their products.

How IoT works

IoT has three components – **web enabled devices, the <u>internet</u> and communication ability.**

The devices are often called _collected devices_ or _smart devices_ and utilize embedded sensors to collect the data and may have components to analyze or process it. Communication components and software send data (information) to other devices, a process called <u>machine to machine (M2M)</u> communication. People may interact with the devices to establish their settings or to view or act on

The Put the YOU in IoT Handbook

---

information. Large amounts of data are transmitted by smart devices promoting the need for faster communication <u>protocol</u>s (the system of rules and standards) and ever greater <u>bandwidth</u>.

IoT Technology

For **IoT** to permit communication between devices and objects certain components are required. Objects need to be uniquely identified. To accomplish this, a <u>Radio Frequency Identification</u> (RFID) tag is used.

<u>Radio Frequency Identification</u> is a term for technologies which incorporate radio waves along with tags in order to identify people or objects.

A <u>tag</u> is a label that contains electronically stored information including its identification "number" and application-specific information such as *batch number* or *production date*. The <u>tag's</u> identification numbers are unique enabling the RFID system design to discriminate among several tags that might be within the range of the RFID reader. The tags are classified as "passive" or "active". **Passive tags** do not have their own energy source; they utilize a nearby device called an <u>RFID reader </u>(a two-way radio transmitter also called an <u>interrogator</u>) to collect energy from radio waves. **Active tags** have a local power source such as a battery and although classified as "nearby" may be located hundreds of meters from the RFID reader. There is a third configuration called **battery assisted passive (BAP)**. It utilizes a battery and is activated when an RFID reader is present. When a smart device collects data, IP networks are used to send it to a database for storage. Database-related processing retrieves the data and presents it in human understandable format.

The term "smart device" is used for a reason. These devices don't just deliver data; smart objects are embedded with both an RFID tag along with **sensors** to measure data. For example, one common use of sensors is to monitor temperature fluctuations. Communication is an important **IoT** feature. However, it need not be wireless. While we usually think of **IoT** as a wireless arrangement, wired configurations also are included within the **IoT** scope. Wired connectivity restricts mobile capabilities.

Government Initiatives

The **Internet of Things** (**IoT**) is evolving worldwide with governments supporting their country's efforts. The United States government has established initiatives to promote IoT in commerce.[1] The US Department of Commerce states:

- "The Department will lead efforts to ensure the **IoT** environment is inclusive and widely accessible to consumers, workers, and businesses.
- The Department will recommend policy and take action to support a stable, secure, and trustworthy **IoT** environment.
- The Department will advocate for and defend a globally connected, open, and interoperable **IoT** environment built upon industry-driven, consensus-based standards.
- The Department will encourage **IoT** growth and innovation by encouraging expanding markets and reducing barriers to entry, and by convening stakeholders to address public policy challenges."

Many countries have released policies for developing **IoT** products and implementing **IoT** usage strategies. The effects of these policies and strategies will impact how U.S. industry competes.

In the United States, while the government supports **IoT**, there is the question of whether regulations are required and, if so, in which areas,

---

[1] Fostering the Advancement of the Internet of Things
The Department of Commerce Internet Policy Task Force & Leadership Team, January 2017

and what should be the role of the individual states. For example, a highly visible **IoT** sector relates to driverless cars. The individual states regulate motor vehicle usage within their borders. However, there is no consensus on whether driverless cars must have a capable driver anyway in case a problem arises and if so what tests or certifications are required for this person. Sensors, such as roadway line scanners, are required to control vehicle operation. However, infrastructure requirements, including those relating to painting scanner-suitable roadway lines, are not established.

The U.S. government is also concerned about security considerations for **IoT** devices sold to the U.S. government. On August 1, 2017 legislation was introduced that specifies minimum cybersecurity standards for this equipment. Executive agencies would have to include specified clauses in contracts for their acquisition.

Blockchain

As **IoT** devices are developed and deployed, companies will make agreements with each other for maintenance, upgrades and services. Since these agreements could be long term, may involve multiple countries with differing accounting rules, and take place in changing development environments, an issue arises over how to ensure that appropriate financial recording occurs, financial changes are recorded and tracked and that contracted payments are made and that no unauthorized changes are made. In addition, there is a concern that a traditional approach using data stored in the cloud on individual data files might be too expensive and not be practical for the multi-billion devices that are anticipated. Also, vulnerability to hacking could be a problem as hackers are tempted by the huge volume of stored data coupled with the ability to enter through billions of points.

One approach rapidly gaining in popularity since 2014 is the use of a type of digital ledger called **blockchain**. Transactions are made in bitcoin or another **cryptocurrency** and to provide appropriate monitoring and review they are recorded chronologically and publicly. Its' architecture is based on a distributed database that maintains a continuously growing list of data records that are designed to resist tampering and revision.

How Blockchain Works

Basically, blockchain is a distributed database with particular characteristics.

Blockchain may be represented as a ledger duplicated a large number of times across a network of computers

It may be thought of as a ledger, or spreadsheet that is duplicated a large number of times across a network of computers and that this network is constructed to update this spreadsheet regularly.

Since blockchain database isn't stored in any single location, the records kept there are public and are verifiable. As there is no centralized version of this information, hacking is unlikely. Because information is stored on a huge number of computers simultaneously it is available to anyone on the internet.

The Effect of Blockchain on IoT

One challenge facing manufacturers is how to manage a device (design updates, third party inclusions, changing contractual agreements with other companies, regulation requirements, such as additions and changes, etc.) over a long period such as 10 or 20 years. Currently the typical approach is to create a database for a deployed device. Associated with this is an update process for handling new firmware and software. A method of keeping track of costs and contractual obligations is also required. This approach can be cumbersome, expensive, and has related security exposures. While blockchain was intended for financial objectives, its use as a transaction processing tool is being considered. Because records could be saved and upgrades could be stored, validated and executed, and cryptography can be used to verify transactions and keep information on the blockchain private, blockchain is regarded as a serious potential alternative.

Sensors

In order for **IoT** devices to work they usually have to detect a change - a change in temperature, volume, light, motion or other physical condition. To do this, a component called a sensor is used. **Sensors** are devices that perceive or measure a physical property and records or reports it. They are examples of devices called **microelectromechanical systems (MEMS)**. Sensors are often utilized with an **application-specific purpose integrated circuit**

(ASIC), a circuit with limited programming capability designed to do a specific task.

Sensors may be used in home or commercial applications and may even be utilized in outside situations. For example, there are applications for a car driver to reserve a parking spot, eliminating the need to drive around city blocks. Sensors designed to detect the presence of a car are embedded in on-street spaces. A smart phone app lets a subscriber know of the availability.
Governments can also use sensors to assist in managing cities. One example: Sensors can be used to detect sound levels to assist in enforcement of noise ordinances.

Multiple purpose sensors and devices
Sensors can sometimes be used in a way not intended by their designers. Apps can be designed to utilize components intended for one purpose in a secondary way making it appear as if they were specifically intended to fulfil this role. For example, a device called an **accelerometer** uses sensors to measure acceleration. However, because of its design it also can distinguish up and down motion giving it another practical use - it can determine road bumps. Used in a smartphone with suitable software to display results and the cell phone can double as a device that can determine the smoothness of a road.

Categories of Sensors
Sensors are designed for a broad range of purposes. Categories of sensors include:
- Acoustical - sound, vibration
- Automotive and transportation
- Chemical
- Electrical - current, voltage, magnetic, radio
- Hydraulics and fluid dynamics - fluid Flow, fluid velocity
- Ionizing radiation, subatomic particles

- Navigation and position - instruments, angle, displacement, distance, speed, acceleration
- Optical - light, imaging, photon
- Pressure and force - presence, density, level
- Thermal - heat, temperature
- Proximity and presence
- *Smell*
- *Health - wearable sensors, vitals monitoring*

Legacy Concerns

The term legacy is used when referring to items that have been superseded but are difficult to replace because of their wide usage, cost or organization related factors. When considering any new technology there is the question for individual and commercial consumers as to whether to convert to the new technology and if so how to determine a suitable migration plan. A significant factor is the lack of strong standards governing **IoT** in general, coupled with a lack of standards relating to specific **IoT** devices. The following chart indicates principal considerations when planning for an update to **IoT** technology:

Considerations for legacy - IoT conversion include

Item	Consideration	Environment
Cost	Utilizing IoT devices may be more expensive than using conventional ones. However, additional capabilities, flexibility or reduced operating costs may make conversion cost effective.	Consumer, commercial
Component availability	Devices (or their components if a device is being constructed) may not be available in all markets.	Consumer, commercial
Compatibility with existing devices	Not all devices will be converted instantaneously (and perhaps some won't be converted at all). Operations in a mixed environment should be addressed.	Commercial
Compatibility with devices from different manufacturers	The inability of some devices to work with those from another manufacturer or developed with different standards affects communication between devices and will affect your overall **IoT** systems objective.	Consumer, commercial
Training	Individuals should be instructed on the overall objective in using **IoT** devices, how to use them, and any procedures and methodologies that result or are changed as a result of using the new items.	Commercial
Change management	Individuals often don't like change from the familiar so plan may be necessary New devices and device upgrades may be introduced so procedures for this should be established	Commercial

The Put the YOU in IoT Handbook

Chapter 2 – Considerations when updating

Technology Basics

In order to update from legacy devices to employ **IoT** it is necessary to understand, at least at a high level, the types of technology that are utilized and how they are applied.

Factors affecting **IoT** can be organized into different categories. These include:

- Communication- communication over a distance which is accomplished utilizing cable, telegraph, telephone, or broadcasting
- Backbone - the portion of infrastructure relating to how different networks are interconnected to provide a path for exchange of data between these different networks.
- Hardware- the physical components of a computer or computer environment such as the machine and wiring
- Protocols- formal descriptions of digital message formats and rules
- Software- the programs and other operating information used by a computer or IoT device
- Cloud Platform
- Machine Learning

The Put the YOU in IoT Handbook

Radio Frequency Identification

Radio Frequency Identification (see chapter 1) or RFID utilizes tags attached to objects to be identified in conjunction with interrogators. As suggested by their name, the interrogators are readers which send a signal to the tags and obtain their information which is then software processed or displayed.

NFC

NFC refers to is a collection of short-range (usually 10 cm or less) wireless technologies. NFC uses an <u>initiator</u> which generates a radio frequency (RF) field used to power a passive target. Since targets don't require power they can have a very simple design such as tags, key fobs, and cards.

.

Bluetooth
Bluetooth is a wireless technology standard for exchanging data over short distances. It uses short-wavelength radio transmissions. Since it unites the telecommunications and computer spaces it is named after King Harald Bluetooth (910–985), credited with uniting Denmark and Norway.

Wi-Fi

Wi-Fi uses radio waves to allow an electronic device to exchange data wirelessly over a computer network. Wi-Fi products are generally designed to conform to wireless local area network (WLAN) standards established by the Institute of Electrical and Electronics Engineers (IEEE).

COMMUNICATIONS TECHNOLOGY SUMMARY

Type	Frequency	Range	Examples
RFID	120–150 kHz (LF), 13.56 MHz (HF), 433 MHz (UHF), 865-868 MHz (Europe)902-928 MHz (North America) UHF, 2450-5800 MHz (microwave), 3.1–10 GHz (microwave	10cm to 200m (4 in. – 656 ft.)	Road tolls, Building Access, Inventory
NFC	13.56 MHz	< 0.2 m (<0.65 ft.)	Smart Wallets/Cards, Action Tags, Access Control
Bluetooth	2400–2480 MHz	1-100m (3.28 ft. – 328 ft.)	Hands-free headsets, key dongles, fitness trackers
Wi-Fi	2.4 GHz, 3.6 GHz and 4.9/5.0 GHz bands	Usually up to 100m (328 ft.) but can be extended.	Routers, Tablets
Global System for Mobile Communications (DSM)	Europe: 900 MHz & 1.8GH US: 1.9 GHz & 850MHz	GSM satellite roaming provides coverage where terrestrial coverage is not available	Open, digital cellular technology to transmit mobile voice and data services. Cell phones

15

Backbone

Cloud computing relates to the delivery of hosted services over the internet. Cloud computing is what allows companies to consume computer resources (for example, data storage) similar to the way utilities (such as electricity) are handled instead of requiring this capability to be built and maintained in house. Combined with communication protocols, the cloud provides a means for interconnection between networks, allowing exchange of data between these different networks.

Hardware

The term **hardware** refers to the physical components of a computer or computer environment. The term refers to computers, their components, physical devices or cables. While components may be mechanical, electrical, electronic or magnetic, when consumers use the term with respect to **IoT** they usually are referring to **IoT** devices or the related systems in which they will be used. Companies usually extend the term to include special purpose <u>sensors</u>, measuring and recording devices and monitors and any equipment used to connect them.

Protocols

For people to talk to each other effectively they should be using the same "language". Similarly, for devices to talk to each other they should follow the same rules. The term <u>protocol</u> is used to denote an agreed upon set of rules that is used for transmitting data between devices. The rules are established and maintained by a centralized standards group. These rules include:

- The format of the data

- The type of error checking to be used
- Data compression method
- The way devices know when a message is being sent
- The way a receiving device knows when a message is terminated
- The way the sending device know its message has been received

The IoT device must support the right <u>protocol</u> to enable communication with other computers or devices.

Software

IoT devices utilize both hardware components and related software. Because it does not require a great amount of processing power C is often used. Java and C are often used for non-complex devices and applications. C++ extends the capabilities of C and is used when the **IoT** device addresses more complex tasks. C# is a higher level of C. Java is a language that is useful when **IoT** device requirements include considerable interfacing and calculation.
Weave is Google and **Nest's** language that is gaining in popularity but is not yet widely used In the **IoT** environment. **Brillo** is another Google platform; it could support Weave.
Apple utilizes its open source language, **Swift**. target marketing iOS and Mac OS developers.
Python is used in web application development. Because it supports embedded programming and is somewhat flexible Python is gaining support by developers.

Cloud

The terms <u>**cloud**</u> and <u>**cloud computing**</u> refer to storing and accessing data and programs utilizing the Internet instead of a computer's hard drive. Companies like cloud because it saves money, is fast and

reliable, scales elastically (I.e.-provides resources as needed), and promotes productivity.
Cloud usage includes:
- Analyzing data for patterns and making predictions
- Creation of new apps and services
- Storage, back up, and recovering data
- Hosting websites and blogs
- Streaming audio and video
- Delivering software on demand

IoT utilizes cloud to connect devices and manage **IoT** data from globally used devices. It supports analysis and processing of data in real time so appropriate action can be taken.

Advantages of IoT
IoT will benefit both companies and individuals. These benefits include:
- Business efficiency can be increased. For example, in both homes and office buildings, automation can be applied to intelligent lighting, HVAC systems, smart appliances and office equipment, building security, distribution of information between offices. Marketing information can be captured for analysis. For example, information such as what a consumer is looking at when they navigate stores can be obtained. Since a store knows what is in a shopper's cart, the need to unload the cart is eliminated and the consumer is charged electronically so the need to stand in long cashier lines in stores and supermarkets can be eliminated.

- Business revenue can be increased. Estimates are that trillions of dollars will be added to the global economy because of **IoT**. Hardware, software, installation and the manufacturing and sales of IoT devices are sources of revenue for companies specializing in these activities. Productivity can be increased. As **IoT** devices are introduced business processes can be less dependent on human factors and will be more efficient. This lowers cost and decreases time to market.

- Business opportunity will be created. New **IoT** applications will be developed and devices will need to be designed, manufactured, marketed and distributed.

- New jobs will be created. As new devices are devised they must be produced and marketed. New skills will be needed. This creates opportunities for the development of skills training materials and courses.
- Home environments can be tailored to reflect individual lifestyle and tastes.

- Devices in the home can be self-monitoring and "fixed" even before they break.

- Individual safety will be increased. Improvements in automobile electronics will result in anti-accident systems. Houses will utilize individual monitoring systems to detect medical, physical, or security problems.

- Objects and machines will be able to send and receive messages to each other, without human involvement. This eliminates errors due to human factors.

- Consumer experience with products will be improved. Products will be able to detect when there is a problem and better communicate the difficulty. Appliances will notify their manufacturer of potential problems so they can be prevented before breaking reducing owner exasperation, inconvenience and costs.

Disadvantages of IoT

Along with significant advantages there are also disadvantages. These fall into three categories:

- Security and breaches in privacy – Devices generally rely on software to work properly. Usually, this software is not protected so unauthorized changes are a concern. When not protected, personal data may be compromised. This can include name, address and possibly account information. Data such as usage information, device location and other information, meaningful to companies and normally not a concern when used properly, could result in loss of privacy or identity if compromised.

- Over-reliance on technology - People are used to obtaining data and making decisions based on that information. With **IoT**, some of that decision making will be made by computers. Depending on usage (for example critical health monitoring or where safety is concerned) these devices are tested thoroughly. However, no equipment is infallible. Assuming that devices won't fail or that the internet is always available with no interruptions and not planning for that eventuality could have serious consequences depending on the **IoT** application.

- Loss of jobs and Social Implications - The use of IoT devices and systems could result in loss of jobs for some people. For example, one IoT application eliminates the need for people to utilize the checkout counter in a supermarket. That will result in the need for fewer cashiers. However, there will also be the creation of new jobs to support **IoT** applications and processes. Usually, new technology results eventually in creating more jobs than are lost; however, new skills have to be developed.

Another area which will be affected is manufacturing. **IoT** technology is being incorporated into the product manufacturing process. It is anticipated that new technology can reduce manufacturing costs up to 50% (panel discussion"Industry 4.0" at TM Forum Live!) as required adjustments to production lines are determined and implemented rapidly rather than requiring completion of a production cycle before changes can be applied. Workers will need to have digital skills in addition to mechanical.

While traditionally companies have offered training, the tendency now is for individuals to self-train. Better educated workers generally have the skills necessary for this so the impact of job shift for less educated individuals needs to be considered.

Determining Needs and Requirements

Determining your needs and requirements vary for company environments and individual usage.

Commercial

For companies, there are many factors in determining **IoT** planning. These may be broken down into three categories:
- Company direction, objectives and goals
- Create devices vs. use devices
- Budget

Company direction, objectives and goals

Within a company projects to be accomplished are chosen because they further the organization's business objective. If a company's objective is to introduce a product a plan should be determined for product development, testing and marketing. If the company's goal is to increase productivity, lower costs and/or expand product lines, use of **IoT** devices should be considered and plans should include determining which devices should be evaluated along with criteria for selecting **IoT** devices and related systems.

Plan for IoT Product Development

There are several overall steps a company should follow when developing a new **IoT** product. Processes to follow within each of these steps depends on the organization's structure and culture.

1. Make sure that a documented process structure is in place. This helps prevent short cuts that could lead to product compromise, promotes consistency between products and helps control development costs. This process should include:
   - Determine product need (market) including its purpose and who will be using it. This should include market segmentation analysis and determining usage of similar or related products and trend analysis.
   - Determine high-level product design including intended product usage, relationship to other **IoT** devices, required sensor categories and related requirements, cloud access capabilities (including carrier dependencies) and software requirements, hardware dependencies, target (rough) price points, in-house manufacturing capabilities and out of house logistics needs
2. Design the device including:
   - High level and detailed technical design (including data attainment, storage, analysis and plans for product technical support)
   - Customer support objectives and plan
   - Manufacturing plan including prototype creation
   - Marketing strategy
3. Create a test plan including:
   - Establishing a test environment
   - Testing that procurement and manufacturing process works
   - Determining a test plan including test cases and testing that product works per specifications
   - Creating and documenting a correction process
   - Plans for testing customer experience/feedback process
4. Develop product implementation plan

- Establish price point
- Create a product launch plan
- Determine a customer feedback plan

Usage in a Commercial Environment

Formerly known as the National Bureau of Standards, the National Institute of Standards and Technology is a unit of the U.S. Commerce Department and promotes and maintains measurement standards. As depicted in NIST Special Publication (SP) 800-183, IoT systems may utilize computation, sensing, communication, and actuation. In aggregate IoT involves the connection between humans as well as non-human physical and cyber objects, and assists monitoring, automation, and decision making. IoT deals with unmanaged devices that connect to a network or the internet.

Connecting to local networks is nothing new; connecting devices on local networks and across the internet has been accomplished for many years. However, there are important new factors distinguishing IoT from prior connectivity:

- Exponential growth – billions of IoT devices are either in place now or will be in the next 2 years.
- Automatic connection – in a marked departure from prior development many new devices are designed to connect automatically to the internet or other devices.
- Security exposure – because of their design most devices have limited or no security.

IoT devices communicate. Therefore they use communication protocols. These include 802.3, 802.11 (WiFi), Bluetooth, BLE, ZigBee, Z-Wave, 6LoWPAN, ANT, NFC, RFID, DigiMesh, WirelessHART, ISA100.11a, EnOcean, WiMax, and LoRaWAN. Although managing and securing 802.11 WiFi networks is well versed for companies, most organizations do not have strong experience with the other protocols.

The Put the YOU in IoT Handbook

Default credentials are often hard-coded into devices, making them easy to compromise. Underlying device operating systems are capable of executing code and in general lack security controls. Unmanaged IoT devices are unprotected and exposed.

Several factors should be considered when planning for using an **IoT** device in a commercial setting:
- Determine purposes and desired features including "must haves" and "nice to have"
- Define how **IoT** device will be used
- Determine training considerations
- Evaluate device security exposures and establish security plan
- Determine reliability history
- Determine support availability
- Determine costs (including purchase and support) and funding availability

Individual Considerations

Several factors should be considered when obtaining an **IoT** device for personal use:
- Determine purposes and desired features including "must haves" and "nice to have". Identify the device need. Store displays and advertising can show impressive charts and graphics. But if the device does not satisfy a particular need then it really is a toy.
- Determine affordability. Compare to similar devices from other manufacturers.
- Determine security and privacy exposures and develop a plan for addressing them
- Determine compatibility with existing environment and devices

- Determine ease of installation and use and related manufacturer recommendations. Some devices might require wiring knowledge to install.
- Determine support availability and types of support offered such as electronic, phone or device-centric (i.e.- the device displays the cause of a problem and suggests a solution).
- Determine if a maintenance plan is available, its' usefulness and cost.

Plan for IoT Product Usage

Several actions should be taken before any IoT device is utilized. These include:
- Determine purposes and desired features including "must haves" and "nice to have."
- Determine device need including problems the device should address. Determine desired features for addressing the need.
- Determine affordability.
- Determine security and privacy exposures and develop a plan for addressing them.
- Determine compatibility with existing environment and devices.
- Determine ease of installation and use and related manufacture recommendations.
- Determine support availability and types of support offered such as electronic, phone or device-centric.

Obsolescence considerations

While any product eventually will exceed its anticipated service life, **IoT** devices are being developed at an extremely fast pace. New features and capabilities are introduced rapidly. One factor affecting consumer purchases, especially in rapidly developing environments, is fear of obsolescence, i.e.- a concern that any purchased product will already be superseded by models with newer features and capabilities.

Obsolescence Planning

Eventual obsolescence of any device or system should be expected. However, managing it is often overlooked – it is often performed in catch-up mode rather than as a planned activity. Cost effectiveness when replacing IoT devices (especially when multiple devices or complex products are involved) cannot be assured without a device update plan.

In planning for dealing with IoT device obsolescence, both companies and individuals should determine those factors which would result in replacing IoT devices. These include:

- Evaluation of new features vs. needs (short-term and long-term)
- Determine if new technology is incorporated and its effects
- Determine viability of continued use of current device
- Costs including purchase price, installation, maintenance and support
- Compatibility of updated device with existing environment (backward compatibility)
- Determine if training is required and if so whether it needs to be formal or self-teaching

Machine Learning

Machine learning is the discipline of getting computers to act without being specifically programmed. When computer systems are able to accomplish tasks associated with human intelligence they are said to exhibit **artificial intelligence** **(AI)**. Because some **IoT** devices (for example, thermostats which are able to determine a homeowner's favorite settings and adjust themselves when his/her presence is detected) exhibit this property, **IoT** devices sometimes are assumed to have artificial intelligence. This assumption is not always valid and the two categories should be considered separately. For example, a detector that measures temperature and reports to a particular smart phone when it exceeds a certain value is an **IoT** device without artificial intelligence. However, **IoT** devices may be used as part of an *AI system*. For example, **IoT** sensors may be used to detect when a car is not following a predetermined route. If they automatically adjust the route to bring the car back to a desired preferred heading the system would be exhibiting AI.

The Put the YOU in IoT Handbook

CHAPTER 3 – Security and Privacy

Communication between devices technology

Background

The term **telecommunications** refers to transmitting information electronically by wires or radio signals utilizing integrated encoding and decoding equipment. The term **generation** is used to denote a particular stage of technological development or innovation. Each generation has associated frequency bands, increased data rates and non–backward-compatible transmission technology.

The **first generation (1G)** stage began in the early 1980's with commercial deployment of cellular networks called **Advanced Mobile Phone Service (AMPS)**. It was designed to carry analog voice over channels in the 800 MHz frequency band.

There was some conflict when the **second generation (2G)** was deployed in the 1990's. In North America some operators used one standard employing technology that could handle up to 64 calls per channel in the 800 MHz band. Elsewhere a standard was utilized which could multiplex 8 calls per channel in the 900 and 1800 MHz bands. **Third generation (3G)** standards were defined to facilitate growth, increase bandwidth and support more diverse applications.

The **International Telecommunications Union (ITU)**, which became an agency of the United Nations in 1947, is an organization whose

The Put the YOU in IoT Handbook

purpose is to promote international cooperation in the use and improvement of telecommunications. 3G is based on a set of standards that comply with the International Mobile Telecommunications-2000 (IMT-2000) specifications by the International Telecommunication Union. 3G was incorporated in wireless voice telephony, mobile Internet access, fixed wireless Internet access, video calls, and mobile TV. 3G telecommunication networks support services that provide an information transfer rate of at least 200 kbit/s.

Fourth generation (4G) provides capabilities defined by the International Telecommunications Union including amended mobile web access, IP telephony, gaming services, high-definition mobile TV, video conferencing, 3D television, and cloud computing. Although the IMT standards set peak speed requirements for 4G service at 100 Mbit/s, this standard is not always followed for communication with items often in motion moving quickly (for example, from trains and cars) and 1 Gbit/s for low mobility communication (for example, pedestrians and stationary users). However, some service providers offer their products as 4G when they can demonstrate significant performance improvement over 3G and are working on satisfying the standards. In designing IoT devices another factor becomes extremely important, the time it takes to send 1 packet of data between devices (called **latency**). Latency is a consideration in the design of commercial uses such as driverless vehicles. With 4G the latency rate is about 50 milliseconds. In 2016, although 4G accounted for only 26% of mobile connections, it actually accounted for 69% of mobile data traffic. 4G connections on average also generated four times more traffic than 3G connections.[2]

5th generation mobile networks (5G) are being developed and tested. They will offer significantly faster data speeds, anticipated at 10 Gbits/s. Latency will be significantly reduced to about 1

---

[2] Cisco Visual Networking Index
    February 2017

millisecond. (In October 2016 Qualcomm developed a chip called the Snapdragon X50 5G modem which supports the 28 GHz band, also called the millimeter wave or mmW spectrum. With 800 MHz bandwidth support, it is designed to provide peak download speeds of up to 35.46 gigabits per second.). Because of technical advances, 5G will permit better **IoT** device and system performance. However there are challenges which must be addressed. Signals at the higher 5G frequencies don't travel as far as they do at 4G frequencies and the signals are more adversely affected by bad weather and obstacles such as buildings and trees.

Backward Compatibility

The term **Backward Compatible** means that something is consistent with earlier models or versions of the same product or technology. Backward compatibility is important because it eliminates the need to start over when upgrading to a newer product or technology.

Traditionally, software was once custom-developed to accomplish a specific purpose. Now specialty code called an *Application Program Interface* (**API**) is written to provide widely useful features. This code enables two software programs to communicate with each other. API design and management are important in **IoT** because how they are developed and utilized plays a significant role in compatibility, as well as exposure of **IOT** devices to customers and interfacing with applications. Release of a new API version is rare. When best practices are followed in API development, often backward compatibility can be achieved just by adding new optional parameters or new methods.

Backward compatibility is more easily accomplished if the previous versions were planned with APIs designed to allow the addition of new features. Such versions are said to be <u>forward compatible</u> or <u>extensible</u>.

Design Considerations

Corporations will use and/or manufacture **IoT** devices. Whether actively engaged in producing specific IoT devices or supporting business operations, companies must consider **IoT** design implications.

Organizations need to consider the following:

- **Performance**. This includes not only a device or system's capabilities but also how well these compare to other devices.
- **Competitor offerings and industry standards**. Similar devices from different companies may differ in features offered, ease of installation, and usage and whether conventional, proprietary, or open architecture is utilized.
- **Interoperability requirements with other devices**. The ability to communicate between devices will determine a device's or system's usefulness.
- **Security** – both inside the company locations, externally and customer exposures
- **Device capabilities** – In addition to interoperability with devices on other networks, ability to work with internal networks should be determined. Also, any network technology has distance and gateway/router concerns.
- **User interface** – If a device is being introduced into an existing environment evaluate if the interface is consistent with other devices in use. If designing a new device how friendly it is to use will be an important selection factor for consumers. Determine whether buttons, LEDs or a display will be included and what web and app interfaces will be provided.
- **Power** – Internal power will determine the tags and sensors being used. If the device will be powered by batteries power usage and conservation abilities must be determined.

- **Antenna** – Wireless devices require an antenna. Portable equipment tends to be made of plastic and the antenna usually is located inside. Metal devices would utilize an external antenna. Antenna design affects device performance and appearance.

Installation and Design considerations

Security

Security for **IoT** devices is a major concern affecting both device manufacturers and individual retail consumers. Manufacturer reputation and sales can be impacted by security breaches relating to their products, and consumers can be victims of pranks, ransomware and data theft. For example, without adequate security it is possible for a malware practitioner to access app code and modify it for "fun" or malicious intent. Thermostats could be ordered to turn on both heating and air conditioning systems causing discomfort and possible damage to environmental systems. For security systems, frequencies could be created outside the normal hearing range of people but which would be heard by animals and result in destructive, annoying or otherwise unwanted behavior.

IoT Privacy Issues

IoT devices rely on the internet which has security issues. Because of widespread and rapidly increasing use of IoT devices there are additional security and privacy concerns.
1. **IoT devices can generate an extremely large amount of data.** This amount is increasing every day as more devices are utilized. In the United States, the Federal Trade Commission determined that found fewer than 10,000 households can generate 150 million discrete data points every day. Since these data points

can provide entry points for hackers they can permit sensitive information to be vulnerable.
2. **Private data may not be private.** Service agreements often must be signed before individuals can use products or services. These agreements often are electronically signed by individuals without being read but they usually permit authorization for information to be shared with the supplier's divisions and corporate partners. This also is the case for **IoT** devices and services. But supplied information can be shared in ways not considered or intended by the person signing the agreement. For example, the signee may wish to rent a car and the rental agency requires completion of driver information. An insurance company "partner" can collect this information, using it when calculating that person's personal auto insurance rate. Other forms of insurance, such as life or health, rates might be affected.
3. **Home privacy isn't private.** Manufacturers or hackers could use a connected device to determine activities being performed in the "privacy" of one's home. For example, smart meter devices could be used to determine the electric appliances being used or the television show being viewed.
4. **Personal IoT devices not envisioned for business use can provide a path to compromise an organizational network.** Many businesses allow, or encourage, employees to work from home and employee homes may have devices not usually associated with business activity. Such equipment can put an organizational network at risk if it is used on a network that works with business assets – that device can be used to transfer control to other devices or computers.

For example, work-at-home employees can be connected to their workplace through VPN connections or the use of cloud services; their home networks usually are not subject to organizational security reviews and testing. Some of these employees could be parents of infants and use a baby monitor, a device not usually found at work. While generally viewed as part of a monitoring or security system, baby monitors are not secure and vulnerabilities, both to individuals and companies, vary by model. Individual example: Camera details from one user may be viewable by another. Corporate example: Malicious actors may be able to utilize their processing power (possibly in conjunction with other non-secure devices) to launch denial of service (DDoS) attacks which can affect organizational performance.

Security vulnerabilities broadly may be considered as falling within three aspects – *attacks against devices, against communications between devices* and *technology suppliers, or against technology suppliers themselves.*

- **Attack against devices** - Devices are designed with a specific objective. Subverting that objective could support an attackers' objective instead. For example, security cameras are intended to protect the installer's environment. When compromised, however a camera system could supply knowledge about the location's physical security to the violator.

- **Attack against communications** – Data being transmitted may be sensitive or the format or amount of data itself may be important to an application. Manipulation of data while in transit could affect its credibility or reliability. Even when the data itself is not altered at a particular time an attacker could determine peak data transmission periods to plan for the most damage due to later interruptions or data loss.

- **Attack against the technology suppliers** - These are assaults against manufacturers and service and solution providers. These entities transmit and process the data which may be proprietary, sensitive or otherwise important to application processing or company operations. Disruption could result in the inability of **IoT** devices to function or to cause them function improperly. In addition, attacks here can affect multiple **IoT** devices simultaneously.

Security Issues

Just because a device utilizes new technology does not mean that older vulnerabilities do not apply. Even new **IoT** devices depicting updated technology may come with components imbedded from third party suppliers. Because of cost considerations these suppliers don't always update deliverables in a timely fashion so older components, even with known vulnerabilities, may be included in new devices.

The following are some vulnerabilities that may be supplied through older (legacy) components:

Legacy vulnerabilities

Local or remote communications are not encrypted.

Stored data is not encrypted.

Command line interface can be utilized

Passwords are not robust and can be easily guessed

The device can be altered locally

The Put the YOU in IoT Handbook

Chapter 4 – Technical Lifestyle

Help Desk Support

People and companies have an expectation that the things they purchase will work as expected. However, this isn't always their experience. Also, environmental changes and normal wear can result in product performance degradation or failure. When difficulties with hardware, software, configuration, appliances, or machinery are experienced, people have become accustomed to looking for on-line support or contacting a manufacturer's support group (help desk). To save money, often these services are provided by individuals living in different parts of the country than where we are situated and are frequently overseas. This sometimes results in language or dialect problems making understanding difficult and resulting in a negative customer experience. To avoid these difficulties, manufacturers increasingly are turning to "built in" diagnostics and support. <u>Lack of standardization on accomplishing this coupled with the challenges and costs of interrupting existing large support structures are problems to be addressed.</u>
One challenge with device support is the need for skill in adding or replacing individual components such as computer chips. To avoid this difficulty, some manufacturers are adopting an updated version of a low-tech practice - constructing devices modularly. Internal software can diagnose component operation, compare to specifications and if results are not satisfactory notify the user to replace the module.

Smart Cities

IoT is a global concept. Municipalities throughout the world are utilizing **IoT** to manage their infrastructure. As this technology is implemented these metropolises are referred to as smart cities. **IoT** is being used to manage parking, street and traffic lights, sewer and water systems and electricity distribution. Cities such as London with large mass transit systems are utilizing **IoT** to assist in passenger flow and even whether an individual is permitted to ride on a vehicle or train.

Security

What does a good Internet of Things strategy include? One of the most important things is a robust plan for keeping your system secure.

84% of **IoT** adopters said they had experienced at least one **IoT** security breach with malware, spyware, and human error being the most common problems. 93% of executives expect IoT security breaches in the future.[3]

Public vs. Private Networks

While seemingly intuitive, in practice the terms public and private can be confusing. They really refer to whether you are using your device in a public setting where anybody may be monitoring you, or in a private setting where you probably know and approve of the individuals accessing your devices. In a public setting you probably want your device usage to be restricted only to trusted users. When you are in a private setting you may be more flexible.

---

[3] Making Sense of the Internet of Things
Ashton, Kevin, 2017

To connect a device to the internet it must have a unique address. A **private IP address** is one that is non-internet facing and is on an internal network. Network devices such as routers provide private IP addresses. They do this by utilizing a process called *Network Address Translation* (NAT).

When referring to internet addressing the term **private network** refers to a **network** that uses **private** IP addresses.

Windows assumes that private networks interface with devices that are trusted. To enable file sharing and other features on private networks, windows utilizes network discovery features to permit other devices to see a Windows computer. When using public networks such as those in stores and restaurants it is not a good practice for the computer to be seen, possibly allowing files to be shared. Therefore, Windows disables these discovery features.

Sometimes users may wish to send or receive data across a shared or public network. A Virtual Private Network (VPN) is a virtualized extension of a private network across a public one. It makes it seem as if the computing devices are interfacing with a private network.

Smarter Devices

The term "smart devices" does not just refer to security, heating and cooling systems, or lighting. Fun devices also are being developed. For example, streaming music throughout a home without the need for snaking wires is possible. There are LED bulb speakers which combine both lighting and a multi-speaker Bluetooth audio. For "mood enhancement" there is a wine dispenser being developed which uses cameras and a cloud connected computer vision algorithm to detect wine type.

Sound experience is also being enhanced. Technology is being adapted to live instruments. **Yamaha Enspire** uses wireless connectivity for pianos.

IoT also is being used to assist in music creation, helping to detect wrong notes and correcting them. Additionally, in the music field, **IoT** technology is being used to assist in live shows where the sound source (music) is someplace other than the theater where the show is occurring.

IoT may be used in the creation and transmission of music over the internet. **Audio mixing** is the term used when multiple tracks are combined into a single track. A mixer board is used which feeds the output of professionally created music to the internet using a device which converts professional grade packets to consumer grade audio.

IoT devices are changing how we keep ourselves fit. The market for wearable fitness clothes is expanding and specific devices are complementing these items. For example, bathroom scales are being expanded to measure health indicators such as heart rate and blood pressure.

IoT technology affecting lifestyle can be seen in cars that park themselves, perform emergency braking, determine when a vehicle is drifting out of its lane, and can even drive itself.

Package tracking using **IoT** technology exists and is being perfected. Both the customer and the supplier can utilize the internet to determine where the package is at any point and determine when it will be delivered.

Optimization and Saving Energy

IoT thermostats are in the process of changing homeowner lifestyles. Using artificial intelligence (AI) techniques they are being designed to determine when different people are in a room and setting room temperatures based on their preferences. Through learned information they determine when heating or cooling might not even be needed and adjust the climate accordingly thereby maximizing climate efficiency and saving money while ensuring comfort. Lifestyle features of **IoT** thermostats now include controlling humidifiers, dehumidifiers and ventilators, and utilize **geofencing**, technology that creates a virtual geographic boundary by using GPS or RFID, along with software that can trigger a response when a mobile device enters or leaves a particular area. Geofencing is also used in lights that turn off when a home is left and turn on upon returning.

Self-Diagnosing Products

For many products it is no longer necessary to wait for a product to break and then call a repair person. Some manufacturers are designing products which not only display the operating condition of the appliance but tell a consumer how to service the problem. While the concept utilizing the internet as it is being applied to new appliances and other products may be considered new to the marketplace, the idea actually was applied decades ago. *On-Board Diagnostics* (**OBD**) resulted from a mandate from the California Air Resources Board. It required that, starting in 1991, all cars have the ability to monitor emissions-related systems. Standard connectors resulted five years later.

Retail Store Support

Commercial apps with increased emphasis on the customer are being established. For example, commercial carpets are being developed containing **IoT** sensors that enable showrooms and stores to determine their customers' traffic patterns. The retailer will be able to present products they wish to emphasize to visitors who also will save time in finding those items sought after the most.

Chapter 5 – The Future

In many respects, when considering **IoT** the future is partly here.

Transportation

Transportation is one highly visible area that is experiencing rapid progress. In the United States, self-driving cars have been developed and tested and their operational considerations (laws and regulations, roadway requirements, user licensing, machine and operator restrictions) are being investigated. **IoT** devices are being implanted on aircraft in support of navigation, weather analysis, passenger comfort and entertainment. Self-navigating electric container ships are being constructed in Norway at Yara International ASA and Kongsberg Gruppen ASA. Initial costs are expected to be high (estimated at approximately 3 times that of conventional ships); however, since they don't require crew or conventional fuel substantial on-going savings (an estimated 90%) could be realized in operating expenses.

In the local transportation arena, how we navigate streets and highways will change. Besides driverless vehicles, street design will be affected. Traffic lights will sense traffic flow and adjust themselves accordingly. In conjunction with these cars will adjust their speed "anticipating" light changes. Some systems are already being tested whereby emergency vehicles can change traffic light colors to clear their path.

Challenges facing companies

The **IoT** paradigm is causing companies to change their perspective of how their operations are performed. For example, a manufacturing company might simply install a bolt. Smart glasses could be used to identify the proper bolt to use. **IoT** capabilities could be used to sense the torque being used for installation and notify the parts inventory system for updating.

Because **IoT** changes and updates are happening at a rapid pace, the ability to respond quickly must be built into industrial **IoT** systems. Existing cultures in older companies which provide for slow change implementation processes need to be re-evaluated. Along with this, the ability to be flexible must be built into systems design.

Support

As devices incorporate self-diagnosis of problems, advise the user on the nature of the problem and how to fix it and incorporate modularity to support ease of maintenance and repair, the nature of the traditional support function will change. Companies may feel that since devices and systems are self-diagnostic the need for help desk support is no longer a requirement. Analysis on whether this is a valid assumption needs to be performed. The need for first level support will change from "tell me what's wrong" to "I've tried your suggestions but they are not working so I am getting frustrated". The help desk contribution of providing customer relationship management needs to be examined, along with additional analysis on data capturing capabilities promoting product improvement and increased sales.

Data Mining

Obtaining, analyzing and reporting data is central to **IoT**. Ensuring that data has integrity is important. The term **big data** refers to very, very large data sets which form the basis for pattern, trend and association analysis. This analysis often relates to human activities and interaction.

Since data can come from a variety of sources it is important to determine relevant and correct data. To do this, data is arranged according to different sources, cleaned to aid in extraction and processing, and prepared for current and future processing. Data patterns are determined and the data is then arranged for reporting in a way meaningful to the user. However, there are several challenges to data mining in an **IoT** environment:

- The need to examine increasingly large volumes of data
- Data come from different sources which may be structured differently making it difficult to compare data between data sets.
- Real time data analysis can be difficult with large data sets

VR considerations and future implications

IoT devices rely on their own processing power. Each device is intended for a specific purpose and when that objective is not immediately required the devices are idle. With billions of **IoT** devices available it is reasonable to assume that at any given time millions of devices would be idle. If small amounts of power from idle **IoT** devices could be aggregated this means that potentially a significant amount of energy could be used for other purposes.

One technology that is expanding is **Virtual Reality (VR)**, a computer technology that replicates a real or imagined environment making it appear that the user is present in that environment and interacting with it. VR is utilized in Video gaming but also in industry as well. For example, in the automobile industry designers utilize VR to visualize how a car would look and function without the need to actually build several designs as well as performing safety scenarios. In medicine VR helps doctors visualize procedures before performing them on patients.

VR environments require power and speed. Aggregated IoT device power coupled with increasing internet speeds could lead to expanded VR applications.

Medical advances

IoT devices are being developed in medicine. For example, people diagnosed with diabetes often are urged to determine and track their sugar levels by sticking themselves to draw a drop of blood that is read by a glucose meter. Anticipate an **IoT** device for determining and monitoring glucose levels. This is important for diabetes detection and opens the possibility that patients might no longer need to stick themselves to self-monitor sugar levels.
In the cardiovascular arena, expect **IoT** devices that will monitor heart activity and detect conditions such as arrhythmia and then activate equipment to correct the situation.
There will be advances in surgery where **IoT** devices will monitor vitals and notify the operating team if there is a situation needing correction and, with authorization, activate equipment to take the appropriate action.

Telecommunications

G5 will lead to an increase in inanimate objects linked together. Lower latency will result in faster coordination between **IoT** devices permitting linking them together creating "**IoT** systems". Much like component-engineered appliances, these systems will be self-diagnosing and faulty **IoT** devices will be replaced without the need for extensive repairs.

Fabrics and Wearables

Wearables, especially sports and fitness items, will undergo large growth. Today, sports and fitness improvement clothing is experiencing market strength because of the desire of amateur and professional athletes to improve performance. **IoT** devices embedded in clothing and accessories such as, watches are available in sports stores and on line. Smart devices can be used to monitor vital signs as activities are performed assisting in monitoring and improving the user's health. Additional detection and reporting capabilities will extend the market for smart wearables and the military will develop martial and civil defense applications.

Jobs and the Work Environment

As **IoT** transforms lifestyle and our environment it will have a strong effect on our job selection.
- Some traditional jobs will no longer be required while other areas will expand. Many retail-style jobs (such as cashier, merchandise display, fixture designing) will decline while there will be an expansion in data analysis and statistical math, software development and jobs requiring quantitative skills.
- Competitive pressures and the need to get new products to market quickly will support the need for more and better trained project managers.
- Security concerns will lead to the need for more certified security professionals. Because negative reviews spread by the internet will affect sales severely, there will be an increased need for product testers.
- Medical procedures will be affected by the implementation of **IoT** devices and jobs relating to procedure trials will increase.

While **IoT** technology will expand in their areas, the need for medical personnel such as doctors, nurses, psychologists, home caregivers and sales people will expand. As new **IoT** devices evolve, new uses for them will be determined so jobs emphasizing creativity will expand. While many smart home-type devices will be "plug-and-play", best use of commercial applications may not be as easy to apply. Learning how to leverage the technology will become increasingly important so teaching and training positions will increase.

Workers will have to learn additional skills and enhance those they currently possess. People generally do not like change partly because what is familiar is comfortable. However, the ability to adapt to change will become an increasingly important worker attribute. An ability to recognize and express new opportunities will be characteristics employers seek in their best workers.

What's next?

It has been estimated that by 2020 electronics for new product designs would include **IoT** technology 95% of the time. [4]
As companies recognize new opportunities to gain customers through **IoT** features and capabilities **IoT** technology will continue to be incorporated into products and processes. It will become increasingly possible to add **IoT** features to a product at lower cost. While security challenges need to be sorted, suppliers should begin to think about how to implement this technology into every electronics-enabled product.

The growth of **IoT** is obvious in developed countries which will continue at an expanding rate. While the growth rate of **IoT** is seems large in the United States, the biggest growth rate has been seen in Asia, followed by Europe.
However, future growth also is likely to be seen in developing areas.
IoT expansion will give rise to business and commerce opportunities. For example, because they use low power, **systems on a chip (SoC or SOC)** are frequently used for mobile electronics applications. These integrate all components in an electronic system into a single chip. It has been speculated that the growth of **IoT** will spur extension in the chip market.

---

[4] Gartner Top Strategic Predictions for 2018 and beyond
Gartner, Inc., October 3, 2017

Security with respect to **IoT** devices and software currently is a concern and related risks will continue to be an issue. Expertise in **IoT**-related security will be required of security certified specialists
New ways of using **IoT** will be implemented. There will be billions of devices dealing with petabytes of data. New organizations will emerge with new applications. Some of these businesses will surpass current companies resulting in a new "business skyline".

IoT standards and practices currently tend to be technical-specific rather than application oriented. Businesses creating products may have to develop different versions of their artifacts. Related costs will result in pressure for standards implementation.

The ability to aggregate and analyze disparate data will be enhanced. **IoT** will play a role in whatever can be monitored and measured.
As more data can be determined, reported and analyzed the ability for more and better human decisions will be enhanced.

The Put the YOU in IoT Handbook

Appendix 1– The How To's

How To Obtain IoT Devices

There are 5 basic processes that are required when considering obtaining and installing **IoT** devices and device systems:
1. Determining your objective
2. Establishing a budget.
3. Determining the devices you want or need, their cost and whether they fit your budget.
4. Obtaining the devices and getting them to work together
5. Ensuring that security risks are determined and mitigated

Determining your objective

Corporations should create a business case and individuals should be able to express the benefit of installing specific **IoT** devices and systems. For devices to works successfully to achieve this objective, it is important to identify the environment in which they will be operating. When devices are being considered a review can be made to ensure that they are designed to operate in this environment.

Establishing a budget

Companies and individuals usually have affixed amount that can be spent without creating financial challenges. Since full-featured devices often cost more, knowing available funding helps limit expenditures and can assist in determining affordable devices.

Determining wanted and needed devices

Understanding your objectives plays a key role here. Knowing the device's purpose enables research (through search engines, web sites, peer recommendations, professional literature) of device

The Put the YOU in IoT Handbook

availability and features and a determination of whether these capabilities address the business objectives and conform to budget.

Obtaining the devices and getting them to work together

Companies often have a procurement process which must be followed for purchases. For existing devices for personal use individuals should:
1. Determine if the desired device already exists and if so which companies produce it. If competitive products exist determine and compare features.
2. Evaluate device and system capabilities against objectives in obtaining the product.
3. Analyze to ensure it works in the intended environment. Determine if personal assistant features work with any other devices in use. If they don't, research whether the manufacturer is planning on joint ventures with producers and decide if you can wait until this occurs.
4. Determine cost. Compare to budgeted amount.
5. Determine if special training is required. Often, usage requirements are included with the product or are available on the web

How to address IoT security
Corporate Environments
1. Devices should communicate only with intended applications. Determine what applications should be accessible. Determine what applications and devices are available both within and on the network. Then review to ensure that they are authorized.
2. If possible use safeguarded private networks to isolate and shield IoT device data from other parts of the Internet and to limit company exposure if device data is attacked. **Wireless access point (WAP)** refers to a networking hardware device that enables a Wi-Fi

compliant device to connect to a wired network. The term **Access Point Name** (**APN**) refers to the name of a gateway between a GSM (Global System for Mobile Communications), GPRS (General Packet Radio Service), 3G or 4G mobile network and another computer network. For a mobile device to make a data connection it must be configured with an APN. If an enterprise utilizes a highly secure local area network, use cellular customer access point names to extend from the data center to remote IoT devices. Additional security then can be provided by organizations by assigning private IP addresses and specifying appropriate authorization levels.
3. Establish a policy that security is a priority topic in **IoT** project discussion and planning. Include security as part of **IoT** strategy and solution planning rather than addressing it as an add-on to an adopted solution. **IoT** affects both the IT and operations areas of a company. Both areas should be represented by individuals with appropriate digital expertise in determining their organization's **IoT** security policies and standards.

Individual Environments
Keep **IoT** devices locked and secured when not in use.

1. Require PINs and passwords to unlock **IoT** internet-enabled devices. Biometric security can add additional protection. (Consider these methods for all internet enabled devices.)
2. In public or other non-private locations use a privacy or blackout screen and shield phone or laptop screens when possible to prevent others from viewing.
3. Use encrypted, password-enabled Wi-Fi. Connect using VPN when possible.

4. Bluetooth is a convenient feature to connect devices. However turn it off to minimize unwanted connections then enable it when necessary.

5. Determine and understand security settings when downloading apps.

6. To help protect against malicious software, download apps from known sites.

How to Deploy a Successful IoT Project

Successful deployment requires development of an **IoT** product implementation plan which includes:

- Establishing price point - used to create financial projections, **establish** a break-even **point** and forecast profit and loss
- **Creating a product launch plan** – the product launch is the point at which customers officially have access to the product and a smooth launch helps establish credibility and promote a customer base
- **Determining a customer feedback plan** – satisfied customers serve as advocates to promote sales, and provide a basis for product improvement

There are several elements that must be addressed when a company is planning to implement an **IoT** project.

- **Analyze needs**. Determine logistics such as the sensors and devices needed and how they will be supplied and methods and design principles that must be followed during both the planning for deployment and deployment phases. Consider special needs (such as distribution factors, geographic needs, team skills requirements and global political situations).

- **Determine best practices** such as regulatory recommendations or requirements and customer feedback processes.
- **Analyze and select solution providers.** Consider items such as data center redundancy, setup costs and availability of pertinent special services such as support capabilities.
- **Determine required data transport techniques** and implementation requirements.
- **Determine publicity/media plan.** A device won't be successful if nobody knows about it.
- **Determine deployment costs and funding.**

Tips on How to Synchronize Whole Home Audio

Within **Alexa** or **Google Home**, configure speakers to operate as a multi-room group. Try using *Chromecast Audio* to connect other speakers having better audio characteristics.

Appendix 2 – Devices and IoT requirements

Smart Bicycles and accessories

Citizen Bikes

Description: Folding bikes using smart phone to display map rides, calories, rip tracking

Requirements: Citizen Bike app

Le Eco Le Super Smart Bike

Description: Carbon fiber or titanium frame with built-in smart phone. Uses Laser beams, activated when front and rear lights are on, to indicate the minimum space a rider needs thereby assisting drivers when passing. Connection for camera. 4G phone shows road speed, navigation, and fitness statistics. Also works as a music player with speaker. Screen is secured using a finger print sensor, which also locks the bike. Rechargeable batteries (externally or when cycling).

Requirements: Runs on Android

Smart Halo Bike Accessory

Description: Provides certain smart bike functionality. Light turns on automatically when dark and off when ride ends. Internal motion sensor triggers a loud tampering alarm. Call and text notifications. Led lights indicate turning points for navigation. Displays fitness progress based on goals defined in app. App indicates parked location.

Requirements: Bluetooth, Smart Halo app.

VanHawk (Warren) Valour Smart Bike

Description: Upscale smart bike. GPS with LED lights in handlebars to indicate which way to turn. Automatic metric tracking. With iOS and Android. Has Gyroscope, Accelerometer, Magnetometer, Speed sensor, GPS Receiver, Mesh-network.

Requirements: VanHawk app

Vanmoof Smart Bike

Description: 3 or 8 speed bike designed for city. GSM anti-theft tracking. Integrated chain lock. Guarantee that if bike is stolen it will be tracked down within 2 weeks or replaced.

Requirements: Vanmoof app, bluetooth

Home Devices

Environment

Heating & Cooling
IOT Thermostats

Installation considerations
Replacing a conventional thermostat with an **IoT** model can be simple. However, different heating systems can be wired in diverse ways and a new thermostat may require different connections from the one being replaced. Often, miswiring simply results in the inconvenience of determining and making the appropriate connections; however, sometimes expensive damage can occur. Tracing thermostat wires back to heating or air conditioning systems may be required. Also, programming thermostats is often easy but some are not simple. Despite manufacturer claims, customer service may not be helpful; we found a tendency to recommend contacting an HVAC specialist to answer simple questions or resolve a simple problem.

Honeywell Model RTH9580
Compatibility: Alexa

Description: Touch screen thermostat for controlling heat and air conditioning. Compatible with Alexa Works with manual (screen) controls, smart phone or voice.

Requirements: Thermostat (multi-colored wires) cable must be present at thermostat location. Works on 24 volts which must be

The Put the YOU in IoT Handbook

supplied through the C (common) thermostat wire. Corresponding C connection is required in the HVAC equipment.

Tip: Some thermostats do not use the C wire. To check if 24 VAC is supplied to the IOT thermostat, after connecting the wires to the thermostat use voltmeter between the red and blue wires.

Honeywell Lyric T5 smart thermostat

Description: Budget-class alternative to Honeywell Lyric Round smart thermostat. Uses touch screen interface. **Works with** with Amazon Echo, Google Home, IFTTT, Stringify, and with the Apple HomeKit ecosystem. Does not work with Wink or Samsung SmartThings hub. Works with single- and multi-stage heating and cooling systems, heat pumps with and without auxiliary heat as well as geothermal and hot-water heating. Also works with 24-volt gas fireplaces. Can automatically determine if heating or cooling mode is best. Supports sending text alerts such as need to change air filyerabout things like when your HVAC system's air filter . **Note**: Does not support humidifiers, dehumidifiers, or ventilators.

Requirements: Requires the presence of the C wire coming from the HVAC system. Relies on Lync mobile app.

Honeywell Lyric Round smart thermostat

Description: Works with single- and multi-stage heating and cooling systems and heat pumps with and without auxiliary heat. Also works with; geothermal and hot water heating along with 24V gas fireplaces; and humidifiers, dehumidifiers, and ventilators. Does not require using C (common) wire, but usage is recommended. Proximity sensor <u>utilized to determine when unit is approached and causes glow.</u>

Requirements: Use of Android or IoS smartphone helps with instllation.

Nest Learning Thermostat 3rd Generation
Description: Compatible with Smart hubs (such as the Wink, Samsung SmartThings, Logitech Harmony}, Amazon Alexa, Google Home,. Made of stainless steel. Nest learns preferred temperatures and programs itself in about a week. Automatically turns itself down when nobody's home to help save energy. with When user is spotted in the room where thermostat is located, lights up to show the time, temperature or weather. Energy Star rated. App shows energy history. Leaf indicates energy saving temperature.

Requirements: Low voltage thermostat (multi-colored wires) cable must be present at thermostat location. Separate device (such as Amazon Alexa) for voice control.

Lighting

GE Lighting C Wi-Fi connected smart light fixture

The Put the YOU in IoT Handbook

Description: Amazon Alexa enabled. Sol LED fixture. WiFi connected. Voice control of lighting. Uses GE app. Functionality of stand-alone Alexa device. Modern clock during the day.

Requirements: U.S. only. Uses GE app

Rxment WiFi controlled LED strip Light

Description: Cutable and linkable LED light strip. Works with Alexa, Google Assistant. Wifi app turns light on/off, changes color with voice control. Sticks in place with 3M sticky tape.

Requirements: Input: AC110-240V (output DC 12V, 2A),WiFi app

Security
  Smart locks

  Considerations

  Smart locks are available with or without keypads. Keypads take door space but add flexibility and reduce key requirements by permitting the assignment of different combinations to different people. Combinations are changeable reducing the threat of compromise and they can be eliminated should an individual no longer need access. Some locks have an alarm for when the lock is forced. Smart locks usually work with smart phones; however some don't. These may come with their own smart phone app and require the use of a separate smart home hub.

The Put the YOU in IoT Handbook

LockState RemoteLock

Description: Receive emails or text messages when anyone arrives. Up to 1000 user or guest codes available. Integrates with Airbnb listing.

Requirements: Connects to existing WiFi router without additional equipment.

Samsung SHS-P718 Digital Door Lock Fingerprint Push Pull Two Way Latch

Description: Compatible with Amazon. Works with any Samsung key tags, or cards. User access code is 4-12 digit number combination. Finger print capacity: Maximum 100 fingerprints, push to enter from Outside and Pull to enter from inside

Requirements: Door thickness: 40-80mm. Power: DC 6V (AA Alkaline Bateries) X8; RF ID: ISO 14443A type(13.56MHz)

August Smart Lock- 2nd Generation

Description: Works with Amazon Alexa, Apple HomeKit, Google Assistant, Android. Voice control with Alexa and the Assistant requires August Connect. Controls door using smartphone. Uses existing deadbolt. Installs inside the door. Automatically locks door upon exiting and auto unlocks on approach. 24/7 activity log on smartphone.

Requirements: Alexa for voice control; existing deadbolt. Voice control with Alexa and the Assistant requires August Connect.

Kwikset Premis Touchscreen Smart Lock

Description: Apple Homekit enabled smart lock with touchscreen. Uses Siri to check history. ANSI/BHMA Grade 2 Certified, SecureScreen, optional auto-lock, optional alarm for incorrect codes, adjustable backset latch 2-3/8" to 2-3/4".

Requirements: Apple Homekit Remote access for monitoring, locking and unlocking requires Apple TV 4th generation or later. Re-key technology only compatible with Kwikset (KW1) keyway

Compatibility: not Android compatible

Schlage Sense Smart Deadbolt

Description: Battery operated deadbolt. Works with Schlage Sense app for Android smartphones, iPhone, iPad, iPod touch. Fits standard pre-drilled doors.

Requirements: Schlage Sense app

Schlage Connect Camelot Touchscreen Deadbolt with Built-In Alarm

Description: Touchscreen deadbolt that works with Amazon Alexa
Requirements: SmartThings, Wink or Iris

Schlage Home Keypad Lever

Description: Lever with keypad, uses Z-wave technology. Works with Amazon Alexa via SmartThings

Requirements: SmartThings – can work with Wink with reduced functionality

Ultralog UL3 BT Bluetooth Enabled Fingerprint and Tourscreen Enabled Smart Lock

Description: Keyless Entry Smart Lock. Works with Amazon. Reversible lever. Allows fingerprint, code, smartphone, shake/knock to open and key usage. Fits both left-handed and right-handed doors. For both indoor and outdoor use. Stores up to 95 Fingerprints and 95 Codes at a time.

Requirements: Optional Deadbolt Cover Plate Required for replacing existing deadbolt

Samsung Ezon SHS-3321 Keyless Smart Universal Deadbolt Digital Door Lock

Description: Smart keyless deadbolt lock. Works with Amazon. Touch pad screen. Adjustable to different door types. Burglar alarm and fire detection sensor. Multilevel security code entry.

Requirements: Can be installed on either right-hand or left side of door but must be defined properly or else will unlock when it is supposed to stay locked (situation can be fixed using manufacturer reset).

Yale Assure Lock Key Free Touchscreen Deadbolt in Satin Nickel

Description: Deadbolt using touchscreen keypad. Replaces existing deadbolt. Unlocks by entering 4-8 digit PIN code. Create up to 25 unique pin codes.

Requirements: . Requires a face bore hole of 2-1/8", backset of 2-3/8" or 2-3/4". Fits on standard doors 1 3/8" to 2 1/4" thick. Can be upgradable to work with SmartThings and Wink with Yale network module (separate purchase).

Bike Security
Considerations

The Internet of Things is providing gear with new technology and features not previously visioned. These include anti-theft devices that provide keyless operation, permit bike sharing, send alerts if a bike leaves a specific area or crashes, and tracks its location. Some devices also analyze trip statistics. **IoT** locks allow the lock to be operated just by being in the proximity. However, advanced technology does not guarantee that they are invincible. Some products have advanced features such as sending an alert if the bike is being stolen. However, they sometimes look expensive, an attraction for thieves when used to protect an expensive bike. The need to recharge power sources is a consideration.

Bisecu

Description: Fully automatic smart bike lock. Locks and unlocks upon leaving. 100 db alarm.

Connectible mounting system. Monitors speed, distance riding time and calories burned. Lithium ion battery has 6 month charge, uses mini USB cable

Requirements: Bluetooth

Bitlock

Description: Keyless bike lock that can unlock via smart phone in pocket by pushing button on lock. Allows sharing. Tracks bike activity. Uses geotagging to keep track of bike location and display on smart phone so locking spot is always known.

Requirements: Supports iPhone 4S or 5, 5C and 5S, 6, 6+, (iOS 7 and 8) and Android phones made since 2015 running Android Jelly Bean 4.3 or later and equipped with Bluetooth Low Energy. No fees for individual smart phone users but fees apply to access BitLock fleet management software for enterprise bikeshare programs.

Elecycle

Description: Smart Lock Anti-theft alarm cable lock for cycling/door/motorcycle. 110 db alarm.

Requirements: Android 4.3 and above and IPhone 4s and above

The Put the YOU in IoT Handbook

I LOCK IT Bike Lock

Description: Automatic proximity bike lock. Charges utilizing micro USB port. Built in 110 db theft alarm. Weighs 1.2 pounds.

Requirements: Uses lithium batteries

KKmoon Bluetooth Chain Smart Lock Anti Theft Alarm Keyless Phone APP Control

Description: anti-theft smart cable lock with anti-cutting, anti- disassembling, removing alarm and vibration alarm. Indoor and outdoor use. 110 db alarm. Lock/unlock via phone app.

Requirements: Bluetooth. Galaxy. Uses 3 AAA batteries, App is called SBAPP.

Lattis Elipse

Description: Bike lock providing automatic keyless access via Bluetooth. Personal 8-character code can be used as backup. Uses solar–charged battery. Sends alert if bike disturbed or crashes. No full GPS capability but captures bike position during locking/unlocking

Requirements: Ellipse app, Bluetooth

Noke U-Lock

Description: U-lock with smart watch compatibility. GPS for parked bike location.

Alarm. Searches for rider's phone and unlocks if found.

Requirements: Bluetooth, Noke app

Sherlock GPS Bike Tracker

Description: Tracks bike location in U.S. and Europe. Installs in handle bars so invisible to thieves. Requires subscription for use after 2 years. Utilizes Bluetooth and GPS module. 15 foot precision. Includes micro USB charging port.

Requirements: Needs battery with 2-week charge cycle.

Smart Bike Lock

Description: Keyless access bike lock. Monitors bike up to 800 feet away. Tampering and crash alerts. Built-in solar charging panel. Dual locking mechanisms.

Requirements: Compatible with iPhone (iOS 9.0+) and Samsung Galaxy/Android (OS 4.4+).

Smart Hubs

Considerations

Not all smart devices "talk" to each other or are even designed to work with each other. When they don't, one solution would be having a device which can control them all. That is the purpose of a smart home hub. Hubs can also be used to make devices look "automatic", appearing to work in conjunction with each other. For example, a door can seem to turn on lights when it is unlocked.

Apple TV 4K

Description: Principle purpose is streaming content to a television; however also serves as a gateway some smart home gadgets. When connected through the Apple TV, Home-Kit-compatible devices can be Siri-controlledSupports 4K content. Has Ethernet, HDMI, microUSB ports.

Requirements: HomeKit, Apple TV

Amazon Echo

Description: Voice controlled utilizing the female-voiced personal assistant, Alexa. Works with devices such as lights, switches, TVs, thermostats, and others from WeMo, Philips Hue, Sony, SmartThings, Insteon, Nest, ecobee, and Wink. Reads news headlines, weather reports, sports scores, news. Links calendar from Google, G Suite, iCloud, Outlook.com or Office 365.. Places Amazon orders. Plays music. Far-field voice control of Amazon Video on Fire TV. Controls timers and sets custom tones for alarms. Free Alexa App on Fire OS, Android, iOS, and desktop browsers. 2.5 inch woofer and 2.0 inch tweeter

Requirements: Supports 802.11a/b/g/n Wi-Fi networks. Does not support connecting to ad-hoc (or peer-to-peer) Wi-Fi networks. Alexa App compatible with Fire OS, Android, and iOS devices and also is accessible via web browser

Tip: Calling and messaging for iOS and Android only.
Hands-free voice control is not supported for Mac OS X devices

Amazon Echo Dot

Description: Voice controlled utilizing the female-voiced personal assistant, **Alexa.** Turns lights and other devices on and off. Reads news headlines, weather reports, sports scores, news. Tracks calendar. Place Amazon orders. Finds and plays music. Can tell jokes when asked. 3.5mm-audio jack and Bluetooth connection.

Requirements: Intended for use with Amazon devices. Bluetooth.
Note: **Any smartphone product controlled via Echo can work similarly with Echo Dot. The main difference between the Echo and Echo Dot is the speaker. The Echo Dot is designed so it can be used with external speakers for more robust sound. A pair of Bluetooth headphones can be linked to Echo Dot.
TIP:** The Echo Dot can be paired with Bluetooth speakers but will not work with a Bluetooth speaker that requires a PIN when pairing.

Amazon Echo Dot with clock

Description: Similar to Echo Dot but with LED clock with adjustable brightness. Device indicates whether a timer or alarm is active.

Amazon Echo Show

Description: Voice controlled utilizing the female-voiced personal assistant enhanced with visuals and optimized for visibility across the room. Alexa. Supports Amazon Video on Fire TV. Works with WeMo, Philips Hue, Sony, ecobee, and other compatible smart home devices.
Shows video flash briefings, Amazon Video content, music lyrics, security cameras, photos, weather forecasts, to-do and shopping lists. Voices Audible audiobooks. Hands-free voice and video calling with an Echo Spot, Echo Show, or the Alexa App. Instantly connects to other Echo home devices. Displays lyrics with Amazon Music. Streams music on Pandora, Spotify, TuneIn, iHeartRadio. Speakers with Dolby processing. Plays music simultaneously across Echo devices (multi-room music not Bluetooth supported). "Drop in" feature allows connection to other units for queries. Eight microphones, beam-forming technology, and noise cancellation,

Requirements: Alexa App on a smart phone with iOS 9.0 or higher, or Android 5.0 or higher

Tip: Emergency 911 calls not supported for voice calling and messaging. For 911 calls, Echo Connect and a home phone are required.

Google Home

Description: Integrated with Google Assistant. Built-in speaker. Works with Chromecast, Nest, Philips Hue, SmartThings, IFTTT, WeMo, Honeywell. Can control Chromecast via voice. Has voice match for individual personal usage. Does not support 911 calls or to premium rate numbers.

Note: There are 3 versions – home, home mini, and home max. Besides price and size, the biggest difference is in sound quality.

Requirements: Wi-Fi network, a nearby electrical outlet, compatible mobile device

Tip: Controlling devices and features requires compatible smart devices (such as Google compatible smart lights, switches, etc.).

Lynky

Description: Google Assitant-enabled touchscreen smart homehub. Blutooth, Zigbee, Wi-Fi, open API integration, native IFTTT support. Can be hooked up with multiple units for large home coverage (2 versions - flat and wall-mounted - powered by light switches; desktop powered by USB). Every Lynky in home automatically connects to each other such that any control or adjustment made to one Lynky syncs to the others while allowing each to have separate "Home Screen" and screensaver / display settings. Comes with 2 microphones and 2W speakers. Security button to place silent mode so unit cannot hear "OK Google". USB Type-C Cable and 120V Power Adapter (Lynky Desktop). Wall model has Wall Mounting Kit for Single-Gang Switch.

Requirements: Wi-Fi, Zigbee/Bluetooth, AC for 5VDC 2.1A power supply

Samsung SmartThings

Description: Can connect to more than 200 devices. Battery backup (4 AA batteries). Downloadable (Android, iOS, and Windows) app enables smart phone to operate as a remote control. Minimum smartphone requirements: iOS 7.0, Android 4.0, Windows Phone 8.1 or greater. Compatible with ZigBee, Z-Wave, and IP-connected devices. Works with: Samsung, Honeywell, Schlage, Yale, First alert, D-Link, OSRAM LIGHTIFY, Leviton, Bose, Cree.

Requirements: Broadband Internet, and Internet router with an available Ethernet port. Indoor use only.

TIP: Range is 50-100 ft. dependent on building construction

Wink Hub 2

Description: 512 MB memory. Works with Alexa voice commands. Dual-band Wi-Fi and Bluetooth. Supports Z-Wave, ZigBee, Lutron Clear Connect and Kidde wireless protocols. Also has its own If This Then That (IFTTT) channel. Power jack and Ethernet port. Has hardware-based security feature (Secure Boot) intended to ensure that only Wink software runs on the hub (thereby making it harder for smart home device hacking). LED strip for status monitoring (blinking blue while pairing, white for rebooting, and solid blue to indicate that everything is connected and working properly). Android and iOS Wink app.

Requirements: Android or iOS

TIP: Wireless hub installation possible, however manufacturer suggests wired connection for simplicity.

Sound

Sonos One speaker

Description: Music player with Alexa natively built in.
Requirements: Multiple devices required for multi-room playing. Coordinated multi-room playing not supported but appears to work with appropriate voice commands.

Ultimate Ears BLAST Portable Wi-Fi / Bluetooth Waterproof Speaker

Description: Portable IP67 rated (immersible to 1 m for 30 minutes) speaker with 360° sound. Works with Alexa voice control. Uses battery with up to 12 hour duration. Wi-Fi and Bluetooth enabled. Updatable using Ultimate Ears app.

Requirements: Battery charger

The Put the YOU in IoT Handbook

Devices and services compatible with Google
[Note: Cell phones utilizing Google and the Android operating system recognize voice commands]

Belkin WeMo through the Google app.
Chromecast, Chromecast Audio, Chromecast Ultra
Emberlight socket (works with Amazon Alexa, Google Home or IFTTT)
GE C-Reach Bridge (works with Amazon Alexa and Google Assistant)
Google, Google Calendar, Google Keep, Google Play Music
Grundig
Honeywell Connect Comfort thermostats
Lyric thermostats (require compatible smart hub to connect)
If This, Then That (IFTTT)
Nest Thermostats
<u>Onelink thermostat</u>
Lux Komo thermostat (works with Amazon Alexa, Apple Home Kit and Google Assistant)
Pandora
Philips
Philips Hue Lighting
Samsung
SmartThings
Sony
Spotify
TP Link Smart Wi-Fi Light switch (works with Amazon Alexa and Google Assistant)
TP Link Smart Plug Mini (works with Amazon Alexa and Google Assistant)
TP Link Smart Plug with energy monitoring (works with Amazon Alexa and Google Assistant)

TuneIn
YouTube Music
Vizio

Devices and services compatible with Amazon Alexa

Amazon Cloud Cam
Amazon Echo (Compatible with select Belkin WeMo, Philips hue, SmartThings, Insteon, and Wink connected devices)
Amazon Echo dot
Amazon Key In-Home Kit (includes: Amazon Cloud Cam (Key Edition) indoor security camera and compatible smart lock)
Green IQ Smart Garden Hub WiFi Irrigation Controller 6 zone
iRobot Roomba 690 Robot Vacuum with Wi-Fi Connectivity

Leviton Z-Wave Enabled 100-Watt LED/CFL or 300-Watt Incandescent Scene Capable Plug-In Lamp Module with LED Locator (Compatible with Wink, SmartThings and Amazon Echo, Requires Wink or SmartThings)

LIFX A60 WiFi LED light bulbs and LED light bulbs with night vision sensor (also works with Smart Things)
Mother and Cookies
Nest Camera indoor security camera
Nest Camera outdoor security camera
Nest learning thermostat Gen 3
NETATMO smart thermostat
NETATMO weather station
Smarter iKettle

The Put the YOU in IoT Handbook

> Somfy all-in-one alarm system HD camera siren
> tado smart radiator thermostat unit starter, valve
> TP Link Smart Plug
> Triby IO smart portable speaker IoT hub
> Triby smart portable speaker with Alexa voice service

Windows IoT Core (Cortana)

Cortana is personal assistant technology introduced on Windows Phone 8.1. Supported on Windows 10 devices, the Speech Platform is used to power speech (Cortana and Dictation) in Windows 10.

An edition of Windows 10, IoT Core is optimized for small-size, low-cost IoT devices. It is anticipated that Cortana on IoT Core will focus on commercial applications. Cortana is enabled on IoT Core in the Windows 10 Creators Update.

Cortana on IoT devices

Cortana can be used on an IoT device. To use Cortana:
- IoT devices utilize the internet - the device must have internet connection.
- In order to utilize Cortana the user must have a Microsoft account (MSA) and is required to sign into this account.
- The device must have a display.
- A microphone and speaker are required for speech interaction with Cortana. The <u>Microsoft Speech Platform</u> Specification provides guidance for the design and development of audio input devices

Devices and services compatible with Apple HomeKit

> Apple TV (4th Gen)
> August Smart Lock

Bryant Housewise Thermostat
Carrier Cor 7 temperature and energy controls
Chamberlain Garage Door Openers
ConnectSense Smart Outlet
D-Link Omna 180 Cam HD Security Camera
Elgato Eve Light Switch
Friday Smart Lock
iDevices Sockets
iDevices Light Switch
iHome Congrol Smart Plug
Insteon Hub Pro
Kwikset Premis Touch Screen Smart Lock
Leviton Decora Smart Switch forApple HomeKit (uses Decora Smart Home App for iOS)
Emerson Sensi Touch Wi-Fi Thermostat
Fibaro Flood Sensor (works with Apple Home app)
iDevices Switch
iLuv Rainbow 8 bridgeless light bulb
Koogeek E26 bulbs
Koogeek strips
Koogeek switches
Koogeek sockets
Lutron Caséta Wireless Smart Lighting Starter Kit
Phillips Hue 3rd Gen light bulbs
Schlage Sense Smart Deadbolt
Yale Assure Smartscreen Deadbolt

Nonclassified

Awair air quality senor (sends smart phone alerts for allergy or asthma sufferers)
Chamberlain MyQ garage opener (works with iPhone or Android device)
Cinder countertop grill (connects to smartphone)
Elgato Eve indoor air/outdoor weather/energy consumption monitor (works with Apple HomeKit)

Eversense smart thermostat (adusts temperature based on smartphone room location)
Fitbark Dog Activity Monitor (tracks dog physical activity similarly to human fitness watches).
GreenIQ Smart Garden Hub (controls irrigation scheduling based on current and forecasted weather), connects to the internet via Wi-Fi or 3 using an app that works on iPhone, iPad, Android smartphone/tablet, PC, or Mac.
Keen Home Smart Vent (Opens and closes room vents. Works with Nest thermostats and smartphones
Lively Medical Alert Watch (Tracks daily activities such as steps and has button to notify Lively to check if a problem arises.)
NETAMO Smart Thermostat (works with iOS, Android, PC and Mac)

Industrial Devices
Consideration: Industrial IoT device operability requirements usually are stricter than those of consumer apparatus. They may be required to operate in hot or cold, dusty, humid noisy or non-smooth mobile environments. Availability of humans to assist in problem solving may be limited.

MachineMetrics Machine Monitoring Solution

Description: Supports factory worker decision making based on real time data. Visualizes real-time manufacturing production data. Provides historical analytics.

Requirements: previous network connection or connection through available hardware kits, access to MachineMetrics cloud

Orbcomm GT-1100 Trailer Tracker

Description: Tracks trailers, railcars, chassis and containers. Uses solar recharging technology.
Requirements: AT&T or T-Mobile network, CargoWatch® web application (for information trailer status, location, history, as well as arrival and departure)

ORBCOMM GT 2300 Intermodal Container Tracker

Description: Self-powered intermodal container tracking system with cellular communications and GPS. Fits within the container. Indicates cargo status, door lock/unlock and movement detection.

Requirements: CargoWatch® web application (for tracking loading and unloading events)

Orbcomm PT 6000 (Cellular, Dual-Mode) Refrigerated Trailer and Container and Railcar Monitor

Description: Two way monitoring and control of refrigerated trailers, containers and railcars. Enables temperature, fuel and maintenance management, multi-temperature zone support Provides event-based alarms.

Requirements: Cellular or dual-mode satellite-cellular versions

The Put the YOU in IoT Handbook

Key IoT Terms

accelerometer – a device that uses sensors to measure acceleration

access controls – processes, actions and devices which prevent unauthorized personnel from entering or accessing a system

accoustical sensor – a specialized sensor that measures sound or vibration

advanced driver assisted systems (ADAS) – electronic systems that aid a vehicle operator while driving

active tags – tags that have a local power source such as a battery

actuator – a device that causes something such as another device to operate

alligator clip – a sprung metal clip with serrated jaws that is attached to a wire for making a temporary connection to a battery, gauge or other component.

angular rate sensor – term used in lieu of gyro sensor. Also called angular velocity sensors

angular velocity – the change in rotational angle per unit of time, usually expressed in degrees per second

antenna – the interface between radio waves disseminating through space and electric currents moving in conductors

app – application downloaded by a user to a mobile device.

application program interface (API)– a collection of computer program subroutine definitions, communication protocols, and tools for building software that establishes communication methods among various components

app controller – a device or system for managing cloud deployed applications

application-specific purpose integrated circuit (ASIC) – a circuit with limited programming capability designed to do a specific task

artificial intelligence (AI) – the theory and development of computer systems and programs able to perform tasks usually considered to require human intelligence

audio mixing – the term used when multiple audio tracks are combined into a single track

augmented reality – a composite view created by superimposing a computer-generated image on another view

autonomous vehicle (AV) – **a** vehicle that can guide itself without human interaction

autonomous levels – grades of autonomous vehicle automation established by SAE International

backward compatible –consistency with earlier models or versions of the same product or technology

battery assisted passive (BAP) tag – a tag that utilizes a battery and is activated when an RFID reader is present.

big data – very, very large data sets which form the basis for pattern, trend and association analysis

blockchain – a system whereby records of transactions made in a cryptocurrency is maintained across several computers that are linked in a peer-to-peer network

bluetooth – a wireless technology standard for exchanging data over short distances

capnometer – a medical instrument which measures the amount of carbon dioxide in a patient's exhaled breath

cloud computing – a general term for the delivery of hosted services over the Internet

cloud security – classification for anything related to protecting online-stored data from theft, leakage, and deletion

cloud services – another term for cloud computing

collected devices – another term for IoT devices

contrast sensor – a high-efficiency device for detecting a difference between two colors (often denoted mark and background)

C-V2X – a technology that enables vehicles to communicate over a dedicated spectrum either peer-to-peer or over a network

cyberphysical system (CPS) – a mechanism that is controlled or monitored by computerized algorithms utilizing the Internet whereby physical and software components operate on different scales, exhibit multiple distinct behaviors and interact with each other in diverse ways depending on context.

cryptocurrency – digital currency utilizing encryption to regulate the generation of money and confirm funds transfer and operating independently of a central bank data analytics – process of inspecting, cleansing, transforming and modeling data to enable discovery of information which supports conclusions and decision-making

data modeling – flowcharts that illustrate relationships among data

domotics – building automation for smart homes

EV – electric vehicle

fly-by-wire – semiautomatic system, which is usually computer-regulated, used to control the flight of an aircraft or spacecraft

firmware over the air – (FOTA) – a technology whereby manufacturers can fix problems or update software after product distribution

gateway – a device that receives information from different points on a network and transmits information elsewhere

generation – a particular stage of technological development or innovation

geofencing – technology that creates a virtual geographic boundary by using GPS or RFID, along with software that can trigger a response when a mobile device enters or leaves a particular area

gimbal – mount supporting sensing devices such as cameras usually allowing the device to move along multiple axes by remote control

gyro sensors – devices that sense angular velocity

graphical user interface (GUI) – the means by which a user interacts with with electronic devices through graphical icons rather than text-based methods

hacking – the gaining of unauthorized access to data in a system or computer

hardware – the physical components of a computer or computer environment

hydraulics and fluid dynamics sensors – sensors used to measure the pressure and flow of fluids such as water.

Information systems security (INFOSEC) –the processes, methodologies and access controls involved with keeping information confidential, available, and assuring its integrity.

internet Protocol Address – a unique address for communication to work properly

Internet of Things (IoT – networks of physical objects with an IP address coupled with the communication that occurs between them and other Internet-enabled devices and systems and utilizes interconnected networks incorporating standardized communication protocol

International Telecommunications Union – (ITU an organization whose purpose is to promote international cooperation in the use and improvement of telecommunications

Internet – global computer arrangement of physical objects which enables people to communicate with each other

interrogator – another term for RFID reader

IoT devices – objects that utilize embedded sensors to collect the data and may have components to analyze or process it and utilize communication components and software to send data (information) to other devices.

IR sensor – a device that detects infrared radiation falling on it

kinematics – the branch of mechanics that deals with the motion of objects independently of the forces which cause the motion

latency – the time it takes to send 1 packet of data between devices

legacy – term used when referring to items that have been superseded but are difficult to replace because of their wide usage, cost or organization related factors

lidar – a detection system working on the radar principle but using light from a laser.

light dependent resistor (LDR) – another term for photoresistor

machine to machine (M2M) – a process where one device sends data to other devices

microelectromechanical systems. (MEMS) – a classification for devices which combine electrical and mechanical components having at least one of the dimensions in the micrometer range.

micropump – pumps with functional dimensions in the micrometer range.

micrometer range – a measurement between 1 micron and 1 millimeter

National Institute of Standards and Technology – a unit of the U.S. Commerce Department that promotes and maintains measurement standards (formerly known as the National Bureau of Standards).

near field communication (NFC) – a collection of short-range (usually 10 cm or less) technologies allowing the short-range wireless intercommunication of mobile phones and other electronic devices

object classification range – the range in which there is sufficient data to classify an object

object revisit rate – the time interval between detecting the same point two times

On-Board Diagnostics (OBD) – the ability of vehicles to monitor systems within the vehicle

optical crop sensor – a device used in evaluating crop conditions by aiming light waves at crop leaves and then measuring the amount of light reflected back to the sensor

parking sensor – road vehicle proximity sensors designed to alert the vehicle or driver of obstacles while parking.

passive tags – tags that do not have their own energy source and utilize a nearby RFID reader

photodiode – a semiconductor diode which, generates a voltage difference or changes its electrical resistance when light is present.

photoresistor – high resistance devices used to indicate the presence or absence of light or in measuring light intensity

piezoelectric effect – the capability of particular materials to generate an electric charge when mechanical stress is applied

private IP address – an IP address that is non-internet facing and is on an internal network

private network. – a network that uses private IP addresses.

probe – (medical devices) – a surgical instrument with a blunt end that is used in investigating a wound or exploring a part of the body

proximity sensors – classification of sensors that can be used to detect the presence of objects surrounding them without having any physical contact

protocol – an agreed upon set of rules that is used for transmitting data between devices

The Put the YOU in IoT Handbook

Radio Frequency Identification (RFID) – a term for technologies which incorporate radio waves along with tags in order to identify people or objects.

remote computing – another term for cloud computing

robotics – technology relating to the design, construction, operation, and application of robots

smart devices – another term for IoT devices

RFID tag – a label that contains electronically stored information including its identification "number" and application-specific information such as batch number or production date

RFID reader – a two-way radio transmitter used to collect energy from radio waves

SAE International – professional organization which develops standards for the engineering industry, with a special focus on automotive, aerospace and commercial vehicles

sensors – devices that perceive or measure a physical property and records or reports it

sensor network – a group of sensors and wireless infrastructure

smart city – an urban area with advanced infrastructure, real estate or housing facility, markets, communication and commuting facilities such that information technology is high and all essential services are easily available for the residents.

smart meter – An electronic device that collects consumption data (such as amount of electricity or gas used) and communicates it to the delivery company and/or consumer

soil sensor – device for measuring moisture levels in soil

spectrum – the range of electromagnetic radio frequencies used in the transmission of sound, data and television

Structure attenuation – the loss of radio wave strength when passing through infrastrucure such as a wall

surface acoustic wave (SAW) – an acoustic wave traveling along the surface of an elastic material such that its' amplitude typically decays exponentially according to depth into the material.

surface acoustic wave sensors – a class of microelectromechanical systems which rely on the modulation of surface acoustic waves to detect a physical phenomenon

telecommunications – the transmission of information electronically by wires or radio signals utilizing integrated encoding and decoding equipment

telephony – the technology relating to development, application, and implementation of telecommunication services in order to electronically transmit electronic voice, fax, or data, between distant parties

telepresence – the technologies that permit an individual to sense as if they were somewhere other than their present location without being actually there.

torque transducer – a device for measuring and recording the torque on a rotating system

tsunami sensor – sensor placed on the ocean floor that measures the change in height of a water column above it by measuring associated changes in water pressure

ultrasonic transducer – a type of acoustic sensor designed to convert electrical signals into ultrasound (transmitter), convert ultrasound into electrical signals (receiver),or both transmit and receive ultrasound (transceiver).

very high frequency (VHF) – the part of the radio spectrum from 30 to 300 megahertz

Virtual reality – computer-generated representation of a three-dimensional image or environment whereby a person using special equipment can engage as if it were real

V2V – vehicle to vehicle communication

V2X – vehicle to infrastructure communication

Wireless access point (WAP) – a networking hardware device that enables a Wi-Fi compliant device to connect to a wired network.

IoT technology changes rapidly. If you would like to be advised of updates to **The Put the YOU in IoT Handbook** email: author@theiothandbook.com

www.ingramcontent.com/pod-product-compliance
Lightning Source LLC
Chambersburg PA
CBHW070418220526
45466CB00004B/1458